A First-Start Easy Reader

This easy reader contains only 33 different words,
repeated often to help the young reader develop
word recognition and interest in reading.

Basic word list for *Animals at the Zoo*

we	going	animals
are	see	elephants
to	zoo	trunks
the	many	bears
at	like	furry
has	big	baby
do	little	monkeys
you	with	swing
can	that	turtles
it	roar	swim
too	come	lions

Animals
at the Zoo

Written by Rose Greydanus

Illustrated by Susan T. Hall

Troll Associates

ISBN 0-89375-271-1

10 9 8 7 6 5 4 3

We are going

to see the animals.

We are going to see the animals at the zoo.

The zoo has many animals.

Do you like animals?

At the zoo, you can see BIG animals.

You can see little animals.

Do you like elephants?

The zoo has elephants.

It has big elephants with big trunks.

It has little elephants

with little trunks.

Do you like bears?

The zoo has bears.

It has big,

furry bears.

It has little,

baby bears.

Do you like monkeys?

The zoo has monkeys.

It has big monkeys
that swing.

It has little monkeys that swing.

The zoo has many animals.

Do you like turtles?

The zoo has turtles.

It has big turtles that swim.

It has little turtles that swim.

Do you like lions?

The zoo has lions.

It has big lions that roar.

It has little lions that roar.

We are going to see the animals at the zoo.

You can come, too!